A GRAPHIC HISTORY OF THE CIVIL RIGHTS MOVEMENT

MEDGAR EVERS
AND THE NAACP

BY GARY JEFFREY
ILLUSTRATED BY NICK SPENDER

Gareth Stevens
Publishing

Please visit our website, www.garethstevens.com.
For a free color catalog of all our high-quality books,
call toll free 1-800-542-2595 or fax 1-877-542-2596.

Library of Congress Cataloging-in-Publication Data

Jeffrey, Gary.
Medgar Evers and the NAACP / Gary Jeffrey.
p. cm. — (A graphic history of the civil rights movement)
Includes index.
ISBN 978-1-4339-7496-0 (pbk.)
ISBN 978-1-4339-7497-7 (6-pack)
ISBN 978-1-4339-7495-3 (library binding)
1. Evers, Medgar Wiley, 1925-1963—Juvenile literature. 2. African
American civil rights workers—Mississippi—Jackson—Biography—Juvenile
literature. 3. Civil rights workers—Mississippi—Jackson—Biography—
Juvenile literature. 4. National Association for the Advancement of Colored
People—Biography—Juvenile literature. 5. Civil rights movements—
Mississippi—History—20th century—Juvenile literature. 6. African
Americans—Civil rights—Mississippi—History—20th century—Juvenile
literature. 7. Mississippi—Race relations—Juvenile literature. 8. Jackson
(Miss.)—Biography—Juvenile literature. I. Title.
F349.J13J44 2012
323.092—dc23
[B]
2011045581

First Edition

Published in 2013 by
Gareth Stevens Publishing
111 East 14th Street, Suite 349
New York, NY 10003

Copyright © 2013 David West Books

Designed by David West Books

Photo credits:
P5t, U.S. National Archives and Records Administration; p5b, Library of
Congress, Prints and Photographs Division; p21, Marion S. Trikosko, U.S.
News & World Report.

Printed in China

CPSIA compliance information: Batch #DWS12GS: For further information contact Gareth Stevens, New York, New York at 1-800-542-2595.

CONTENTS

Following the rise of "Jim Crow" segregation laws in the South, African Americans found themselves increasingly cut off from the vote during the 1890s.

A group of outspoken African Americans and whites began meeting to work out how to help these disenfranchised "people of color." In 1909, the National Association for the Advancement of Colored People was born.

Harvard scholar W.E.B. DuBois was a key founding member of the NAACP.

A 1911 edition of the NAACP magazine —The Crisis

STANDING TOGETHER

During the 1920s and 1930s, the NAACP campaigned against lynching (unlawful, mob-driven executions of African Americans) by publicizing cases. They fought segregation laws through the courts and strove to overcome the obstacles that had been put in place to deny African Americans representation in the Southern states.

Ninteen-year-old Medgar Wiley Evers fought in Europe during World War II.

"NEVER BE ASHAMED OF WHO YOU ARE."

Farmer James Evers was unusual among most African American residents of Decatur, Mississippi, in owning his own land. He was also fiercely proud, a quality he passed on to his third child, Medgar.

Medgar earned his high school diploma and joined the army in 1943. In 1946, he returned from the war to go to college. Soon he began to get involved with the NAACP, a role that would prove to have terrible personal consequences…

5

Medgar Evers and the
NAACP

THE MORNING OF JUNE 11, 1963, MARGARET WALKER ALEXANDER DRIVE, JACKSON, MISSISSIPPI.

AS HIS WIFE, MYRLIE, TURNED TO GO BACK INSIDE, MEDGAR EVERS PAUSED AND STARED AT THE OVERGROWN VACANT LOT ACROSS THE STREET.

SOMETHING ABOUT THAT SPACE...WORRIES ME...

WEARILY, HE LOWERED HIMSELF INTO THE CAR.

EVERS'S JOURNEY AS A CIVIL RIGHTS CRUSADER HAD BEGUN BACK IN 1946...

VROOOOM!

...WHEN HE, HIS BROTHER, AND A FEW OTHER EX-SOLDIERS HAD ACTUALLY DARED TO REGISTER TO **VOTE**...

UH-OH, IT LOOKS LIKE WE'VE GOT A WELCOMING COMMITTEE.

POLLING STATION

A POSSE OF ARMED WHITES STOOD GUARD ON THE DECATUR COURTHOUSE STEPS.

9

AT A TIME WHEN MOST YOUNG FATHERS WOULD BE CONCERNED WITH EARNING A LIVELIHOOD, EVERS **STOOD UP** AT A LOCAL MEETING OF THE NAACP AND ANNOUNCED...

I VOLUNTEER TO APPLY TO **MISSISSIPPI STATE UNIVERSITY!**

THE NAACP HAD SEVERAL ONGOING CASES CHALLENGING SCHOOL SEGREGATION. EVERS SAW A CHANCE TO TAKE ON JIM CROW IN MISSISSIPPI.

ALTHOUGH UNSUCCESSFUL, EVERS'S BID TO ENROLL AT "OLE MISS" GOT HIM RECOGNIZED BY THE NAACP LEADERSHIP, WHO APPOINTED HIM THEIR *FIRST MISSISSIPPI STATE FIELD SECRETARY,* BASED IN JACKSON...

...SO YOU SEE, MR. EVERS, BECAUSE *I'VE* ENROLLED IN THE NAACP, THE *WHITE FOLKS* WHO *RUN* THE BANK HAVE *CALLED IN* MY LOAN.

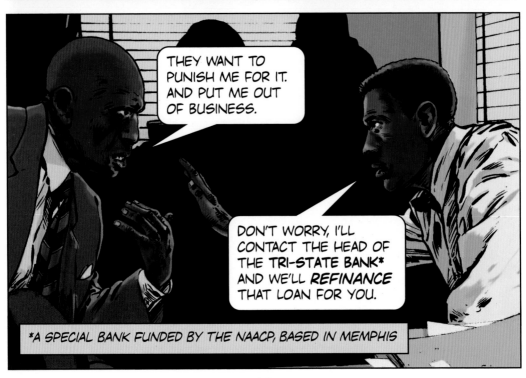

THEY WANT TO PUNISH ME FOR IT. AND PUT ME OUT OF BUSINESS.

DON'T WORRY, I'LL CONTACT THE HEAD OF THE *TRI-STATE BANK** AND WE'LL *REFINANCE* THAT LOAN FOR YOU.

*A SPECIAL BANK FUNDED BY THE NAACP, BASED IN MEMPHIS

LIKE HIS FATHER BEFORE HIM, A MAN WHO REFUSED TO GIVE WAY WHEN MEETING WHITES ON THE SIDEWALK, EVERS WON A GRUDGING **RESPECT** FROM MANY WHITES. THIS **ALLOWED** HIM TO GO ABOUT HIS BUSINESS...

...WORKING TIRELESSLY TO SECURE FREEDOM FOR HIS **CHILDREN'S** GENERATION.

JAMES VAN

DARRELL KENYATTA

REENA DENISE

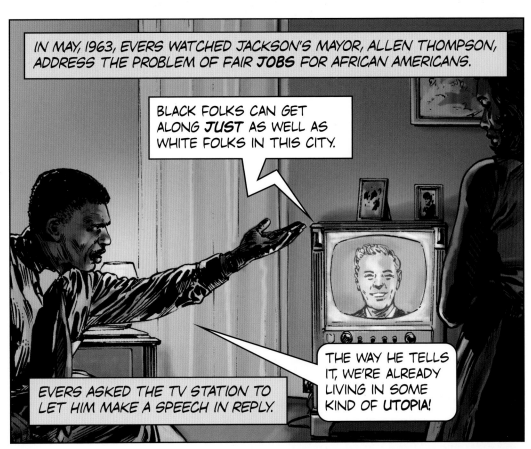

IN MAY, 1963, EVERS WATCHED JACKSON'S MAYOR, ALLEN THOMPSON, ADDRESS THE PROBLEM OF FAIR **JOBS** FOR AFRICAN AMERICANS.

BLACK FOLKS CAN GET ALONG **JUST** AS WELL AS WHITE FOLKS IN THIS CITY.

EVERS ASKED THE TV STATION TO LET HIM MAKE A SPEECH IN REPLY.

THE WAY HE TELLS IT, WE'RE ALREADY LIVING IN SOME KIND OF **UTOPIA!**

HIS REPUTATION WAS SUCH THAT THEY AGREED **AND** GAVE HIM THE SAME NUMBER OF MINUTES.

A BLACK IN THE NEW NATION OF CONGO CAN BE A TRAIN ENGINEER, BUT IN **JACKSON**, HE CAN'T EVEN DRIVE A **GARBAGE TRUCK!**

WE PLAN TO **INCREASE** OUR DEMONSTRATIONS UNTIL JIM CROW IS COMPLETELY **ERADICATED** FROM JACKSON, MISSISSIPPI.

THE CIVIL RIGHTS MOVEMENT HAD STARTED USING **DIRECT ACTION,** LIKE LUNCH COUNTER SIT-INS, TO CHALLENGE SEGREGATION.

IN THE EARLY HOURS OF MAY 29, A HOMEMADE FIREBOMB WAS THROWN INTO THE EVERSES' CARPORT.

EVERS WAS USED TO BEING NAMED ON SO-CALLED DEATH LISTS, BUT THIS WAS SOMETHING MORE.

DURING THE EVENING OF JUNE 11, AS MEDGAR WORKED LATE, MYRLIE WATCHED PRESIDENT KENNEDY'S ADDRESS ON THE UPCOMING CIVIL RIGHTS BILL.

"NOW THE TIME HAS COME FOR THIS NATION TO FULFILL ITS PROMISE. THE EVENTS IN BIRMINGHAM AND ELSEWHERE HAVE SO INCREASED THE CRIES FOR EQUALITY THAT NO CITY OR STATE OR LEGISLATIVE BODY CAN PRUDENTLY CHOOSE TO IGNORE THEM."

JUST AFTER MIDNIGHT, EVERS PULLED INTO HIS DRIVEWAY.

AS HE BENT DOWN TO FETCH ITEMS FROM THE BACK SEAT, ON THE VACANT LOT ACROSS THE STREET, A GUNMAN RAISED A RIFLE...

...AND TOOK AIM.

CRACK!

THE HIGH-POWERED BULLET PIERCED HIS UPPER BACK, PITCHING HIM FORWARDS.

HNNNNGH!

MEDGAR!

EVERS HAD MANAGED TO CRAWL TO THE FRONT STEP.

DADDY! DADDY! GET UP!

FIFTY MINUTES LATER, HE WAS DEAD.

THE FIRST NATIONAL CIVIL RIGHTS LEADER TO BE ASSASSINATED, EVERS'S DEATH SHOCKED BLACK AND WHITE SOCIETY ALIKE.

After Evers's killing, and led by his brother Charlie, those fighting the civil rights battle in Mississippi redoubled their efforts. In 1969, Charles Evers became the first African American mayor of a Mississippi city since the 1870s.

Evers helped pave the way for James Meredith to become the first African American student to attend the previously segregated Mississippi State University in 1962. Meredith's first day at the college sparked a riot.

Time Catches Up

The rifle used to kill Evers was found to have fingerprints on it belonging to Byron De La Beckwith, a fertilizer salesman with connections to the White Citizens Council of Jackson.

De La Beckwith was quickly arrested, but a trial and a retrial by all-white juries produced a hung verdict. It took until 1994 to finally serve justice on Evers's killer, who died in prison in 2001.

An Unsung Hero

When asked why he didn't take more credit for his achievements, Evers said, "It's not about me, it's about the little people." Overshadowed for years by more famous civil rights leaders, Evers has come to be memorialized on a warship, a university campus, and in various parts of Jackson, Mississippi.

Evers was buried at Arlington Cemetery with full military honors.

GLOSSARY

crusader A person who speaks out and fights for a cause.

disenfranchised Denied rights, especially the right to vote.

eradicated Eliminated, driven out.

executions Public killings, usually of criminals.

grudging Reluctant or unwilling.

hung verdict A decision in a court case in which the jury cannot agree whether the defendant is guilty or innocent.

posse A large group gathered to act together.

prudently Wisely.

refinance Get a different lender of a loan.

segregation The forced separation of whites and blacks in public.

status quo The way things are currently done.

supremacists Those who believe that one group of people is better than, or superior to, another group.

utopia An ideal, perfect society.

vacant Empty, uninhabited.

INDEX